How Not
to Kill Your
BABY

Kids are like a mirror, what they see
and hear they do. Be a good reflection
for them. Enjoy your little one, because
they really do grow up too fast!
The most important advice I can
give you is to not be too serious. Be
silly, be fun and enjoy all the
wonderful moments ahead with your
little girl. Congratulations, Diane
Cline

OTHER BOOKS BY
JACOB SAGER WEINSTEIN

- - - - - - - - - - - - -

The Government Manual for New Superheroes
(with Matthew David Brozik)

The Government Manual for New Wizards
(with Matthew David Brozik)

The Government Manual for New Pirates
(with Matthew David Brozik)

How Not to Kill Your BABY

The Revolutionary New Way to Raise Perfect Children, Get Them into a Good Med School, Keep Them Safe from Ever Being Sad About Anything, and, Oh, Who Are We Kidding? It's a Parody.

JACOB SAGER WEINSTEIN

Andrews McMeel
Publishing, LLC

Kansas City · Sydney · London

Andrews McMeel Publishing, LLC
an Andrews McMeel Universal company
1130 Walnut Street, Kansas City, Missouri 64106
www.andrewsmcmeel.com

12 13 14 15 16 TEN 10 9 8 7 6 5 4 3 2 1
ISBN: 978-1-4494-0991-3
Library of Congress Control Number: 2011932654

Book Design by Diane Marsh

ATTENTION: SCHOOLS AND BUSINESSES
Andrews McMeel books are available at quantity discounts with bulk purchase for educational, business, or sales promotional use. For information, please e-mail the Andrews McMeel Publishing Special Sales Department: specialsales@amuniversal.com

Your child's safety is your responsibility. Read these safety warnings and keep them in mind **at all times**, even while sleeping.

Book may present tripping hazard if left on ground.

Audio version of book may cause hearing loss if played at excessive volume.

1. Never leave your child unattended with a book.

2. **Choking hazard** if your child has a large, book-shaped mouth.

3. **Risk of electrocution.** Do not read this book while flying a kite outside in an electrical storm standing with both feet in a bucket of salt water.

4. **ALLERGY WARNING:** This book is printed in a facility that also prints *Peanuts*.

5. This book is **not a toy.** Do not put little lips on the side, then open and close the covers to make it speak.

6. This book is an **FCC Class M device,** and may cause interference if read aloud when the person next to you is trying to use the telephone.

Transporting more than thirty copies of book in carry-on luggage may result in extra baggage handling fees, but it's totally worth it.

Reading of this book or other materials in a ring of fire may burn, burn, burn.

7. This book complies with all FAA regulations. It is safe to use on an airplane, unless you have purchased the special limited edition hewn from solid diamond, in which case, corners of book may cut airplane windows, resulting in **sudden loss of cabin pressure**.

8. **Do not read the following sentence while driving,** as the display of filial affection may cause eye watering and subsequent **impairment of vision:** This book is **dedicated to my parents**, with love and gratitude.

9. Do not permit children to tie book around neck for use as a superhero cape. **Book does not enable user to fly.**

CONTENTS

-- -- -- -- -- -- -- -- -- -- -- -- --

FREE BONUS:
Official How Not to Kill Your Baby™ Baby-Proofing Kit
111

INTRODUCTION

Dear Parents-to-Be,[1]

Ever since you received the good news, you've been subjected to an endless barrage of bad news, from dire warnings of dietary health risks to incessant pressure to follow the latest trendy parenting fad.

This book is written in the commonsense belief that, no matter how much pressure society puts on you, it's always possible to add more. *Tons* more. Hundreds of pages more, plus illustrations.

So, read on.

Unless you're some kind of baby-hating creep who wants to parent all wrong.

---

1   Or, if you have taken the very sensible precaution of reading this book before getting pregnant, "Parents-to-be-to-be."

Birth to puberty:
Conception impossible unless you are some kind of medical freak.

Teen years:
Conception only suitable for bad girls who want to ruin their futures.

Twenties:
Conception only suitable for flighty airheads who don't think about their careers.

Thirties: *Increased risk of birth defects. Conception only suitable for selfish working women who think of nothing but their own careers.*

Exactly on your twentieth birthday: Bingo!

CHAPTER 1

Things to Worry About Before Getting Pregnant

When Should You Conceive?

Choosing *when* to get pregnant is the very first decision you will make as a parent. Take a look at this time line.

Forties: *Natural conception virtually impossible. Parenthood requires unholy scientific meddling.*

Fifties through death: *Conception completely impossible. Plus, you've missed out on your chance for grandchildren.*

A casual glance at the timeline may suggest there is *no* good time to bear children. But look more closely. There—right between the teens and twenties:

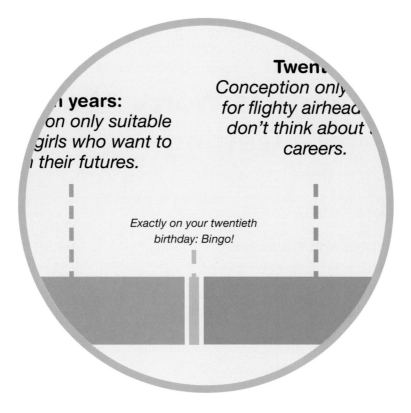

Exactly on your twentieth
birthday: Bingo!

years:
on only suitable
girls who want to
their futures.

Twent...
Conception only
for flighty airhead...
don't think about...
careers.

That's right: The only correct time to get pregnant is on your twentieth birthday. And we mean *exactly*. If you were born at 4 a.m. on June 28 and you wait until 4:01 a.m., you've missed your chance and you shouldn't even bother.[1]

---

1   And, needless to say, we can't advise you to conceive ten seconds *before* your twentieth birthday, because what kind of sicko condones teen pregnancy?

Using Alternative Methods of Conception

For some couples, conceiving a child through intercourse may prove difficult. If traditional, missionary-style intercourse doesn't do the trick, don't be afraid to try different positions, or locations, or sexual acts, which might not seem procreative and might even seem anti-procreative, because what if that was it? New science also suggests that fertility appears to benefit from a "performance effect" if videotaped.

If these additional techniques do not bring success, you may be tempted to use an alternative method of conception. Before you take this drastic and highly risky action, please consider the following table.

Six Examples of People Who Were Born Through Alternative Methods of Conception or Delivery and the Terrifying Consequences for Everybody Involved

NAME	ALTERNATIVE METHOD	TERRIFYING CONSEQUENCE
Louise Brown	World's first conception through in vitro fertilization	At age thirty-four, has yet to win a single Olympic gold medal.
Dolly the Sheep	Cloning	Born with hooves instead of hands or feet.
Alien Chest Exploding Thingy	Implanted in chest of innocent spaceman	Killed repeatedly by Sigourney Weaver.
Julius Caesar	Caesarian section	Forced to learn Latin from birth. Also, eventually, stabbed to death.

continued

NAME	ALTERNATIVE METHOD	TERRIFYING CONSEQUENCE
Superman	Wrapped in swaddling cloth and blasted into outer space	Mother, father, and entire home planet destroyed in massive explosion.
Jesus Christ	Immaculate	Dead at age thirty-three.

Conceiving by Rubbing Two Delicate Body Parts That Are Highly Sensitive to Pain Against Each Other

Now that you know the horrible dangers of any method other than traditional intercourse, it is time to contemplate the horrible dangers of traditional intercourse. These include:

Sexually transmitted diseases. Fortunately, these are easy to avoid. Since no known STD has an incubation period longer than ten years, simply take the common-sense precaution of locking your partner in a chastity belt for a decade before so much as holding hands.

Chastity belts (his and hers)

WARNING: Babies who emerge fully grown from giant oyster shells are at high risk for developing salmonella.

Since the correct age to conceive is twenty, choosing your partners ten years in advance requires being engaged at age ten. See the sidebar for tips on how to do this.

Emotional attachment. Orgasm results in the release of a hormone known as "oxytocin," which stimulates feelings of well-being and contentment. These emotions are probably harmless, unless, of course, they lower your alertness so much that you fail to notice your house is on fire, in which case, they will kill you. More alarmingly, oxytocin stimulates emotional attachment, which is why every time you have sex, you put yourself at risk of falling for a good-looking loner who has seduced you only to frame you for murder.

"Hi, honey. I brought you some flowers. Oh, and would you mind putting your fingerprints on this handgun?"

CHOOSING THE PERFECT PARENT

Yes, picking the future father or mother of your child from among your fellow fourth-graders may be a challenge. But it is one you must undertake if you hope to one day know the joy of seeing your own ten-year-old child engaged to a loving and supportive life partner. Here's a quick visual guide to help you choose the future mother or father of your child:

Pros: Fun loving and artistic.
Cons: Those hands may be genetic.

Pros: Thoughtful and quiet.
Cons: Even a decade later, trace elements of dandelion pollen may cause anaphylactic shock in newborns.

Pros: Likely to father future Nobel Prize winners.
Cons: Likely to father future victims of playground bullying.

Physical attachment. Sexual intercourse can lead to a condition known as coitus captivus, in which the man and woman are unable to detach themselves after climax. Your doctor will no doubt tell you he has never seen a case of this and doubts it is even possible, but ask yourself this: *If it weren't possible, why would they have a name for it?*

Melvin and Betty have been stuck together since 1964.

Eternal damnation. Virtually every major religion agrees: Intercourse outside of marriage results in eternal damnation for both partners. But did you know that it can also result in damnation for any resulting children, according to many faiths, which nobody can prove are false? Before any sexual contact, you will therefore want to take the following simple precautions:

1. Get out your marriage license and confirm that the signature of the officiating clergy member has not faded; if it has, your marriage is no longer valid in the eyes of the Lord.

2. Hire a private detective to investigate the officiant to ensure that you were not married by a zany morning-zoo DJ who was only pretending to be a priest for the amusement of his listeners.

3. Contact your local government to confirm that gay marriage has not been legalized in your area, as a single gay marriage is enough to desanctify every heterosexual relationship within a hundred miles. If you are downstream from any godless cities or states, gay marriage may even have leaked into your water supply, which means that you could literally be bathing in sin. Consider having a water filter installed; make sure that it has an activated carbon outtake chamber and an intake valve made out of a pure communion wafer.

DAN'S TIPS FOR DADS-TO-BE

— — — — —

Hi there! My name is Dan, and if you're anything like me, you're a guy! And that means that you can't possibly understand anything about pregnancy unless it has lots of sports metaphors and exclamation marks!

That's why the eggheads who wrote this book have brought me in as a pinch hitter. Only instead of waiting for "the bottom of the ninth," I'm coming in at "the top of the first"—the first month, that is! Of pregnancy! Specifically, your wife's pregnancy! (With me so far? Do you need more exclamation points or anything? No? Great!)

Now, they're still going to include information for dads in the main body of the text, but don't worry! Whenever things get too complicated for knuckleheaded lunks like you and me, I'll pop up to give the play-by-play. Just think of me as the John Madden of your wife's hoo-ha! Good luck, and see you soon!

Adoption

As you can see, however you choose to conceive a child, you are probably doing it wrong. You may, therefore, be tempted to let somebody else do it for you. You may, in other words, wish to adopt, giving a child the safe and loving home he would otherwise never know, and passing on to him the wisdom and values that are so much more valuable than any genetic inheritance. This can only end badly.

SOURCE OF INFANT	WHAT HE OR SHE WILL DO WHEN OLDER
Adopted from an orphanage	Become enmeshed in an ornate plot involving virtuous flower girls, roguish chimney sweeps, conniving bankers, and at least one secret codicil to a millionaire's will.
Taken in after surviving an encounter with He Who Must Not Be Named	Lead friends into battle against Dark Lord, resulting in numerous deaths and sizable damage to school property.
Fished out of the river Nile	Lead the Jews out of Egypt, setting in motion a complex chain of events that, millennia later, will make it much harder for Gentiles to get jobs as orthodontists.

Conclusions

The earliest stage of the reproductive process is a time of anticipation and hope, but it can also be one of fear and concern. By now, though, you should know that there's nothing to worry about, as long as you don't obtain your child through sex, through science, or through adoption. Good luck, and remember: The important thing is to enjoy the journey!

Even if it's a journey down a bottomless pit filled with horrors.

- - - - - - - - -

CHAPTER 2

How Not to Kill Your Fetus

Congratulations! You're Pregnant!

At least, you *might* be pregnant, because the most common signs of pregnancy are also symptoms of horrible diseases.

SYMPTOM	POSSIBLE OTHER CAUSE
Frequent urination	Diabetes.
Morning sickness	Cancer.
Strange food cravings	The foods you usually eat taste unpleasant because your good-looking loner husband is slipping arsenic into them. Also, tongue cancer.
Frequent urination, morning sickness, *and* strange food cravings	Hysterical pregnancy.
Frequent urination, morning sickness, and strange food cravings *plus* a positive result on a pregnancy test	Hysterical pregnancy so extreme, you have sucked the entire pharmaceutical industry into your neurotic web of self-deception.

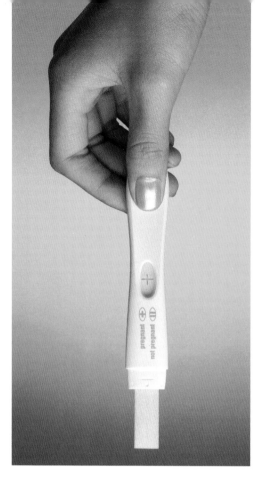

Congratulations! You're pregnant! Or clinically insane!

If you have any of the above symptoms, put down this book at once and call your doctor, even if he's in Hawaii celebrating his twenty-fifth wedding anniversary. If he insists that your symptoms are healthy signs of a normal pregnancy, keep calling him until he acknowledges that you're horribly ill and there's nothing he can do for you, possibly using the phrase "For God's sake, stop calling! You're making me yell and it's scaring the fire dancers!" This is simply a technical medical term that means "I'm sorry to tell you this, but you're going to die."

However, assuming your pregnancy isn't accompanied by morning sickness, frequent urination, food cravings, or a positive pregnancy test, you have nothing to worry about. Please feel free to read the rest of this chapter.

Proper fork placement for women carrying quadruplets

Nutrition During Pregnancy

For the next nine months, every time you sit down to eat a meal, you'll need to remember that you're eating for two. That means you'll need to use twice as much silverware.

It also means you'll need to exhaustively research the nutritional impact of everything you put in your mouth, including any stray molecules you inhale. For this reason, make sure that you carry a mass spectrometer with you at all times.

Larger items of food may safely be identified purely by visual means. Simply refer to this guide.

These strawberries are an excellent source of vitamin C and flavonoids.

These strawberries are coated with deadly pesticide.

These grapes are a good source of resveratrol and other phytochemicals.

These grapes are coated with deadly pesticide.

These bananas are an excellent source of vitamin C.

These bananas are coated with deadly pesticide, but you may simply remove the peels, at which point, they will become slip-and-fall hazards that will kill you long before the pesticide gets the chance. Also, there may be spiders.

Other Hazards

Cell Phones

Although no reputable studies have suggested that cell phone use is hazardous during pregnancy, we feel it is worth mentioning that we knew this one lady who used her cell phone all the time, and her baby came out with a soft spot right on the top of his head, so it may be wise to take suitable precautions.

Correct use of a cell phone during pregnancy

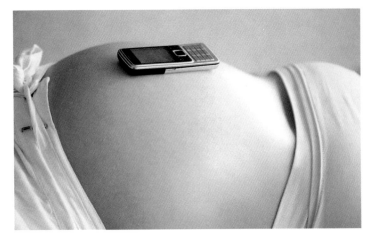

Incorrect use

Television

Did you ever sit less than three feet away from the TV? If so, start saving up for a lifetime of corrective lens purchases, because this is what your children are going to look like:

Please note that the three-feet rule describes the distance between the television set and the far end of the relevant reproductive organ. Men, therefore, must sit three feet away, *plus an additional distance depending on the length of the penis.* Assuming an average penis size of 11.5 inches, the minimum safe distance for men is about four feet.

Every time he got excited, Roderick had to move an additional eighteen inches away from the TV.

SPECIAL EDITIONS

— — — — —

At How Not to Kill Your Baby Publications, Amalgamated, the safety of your baby is our highest concern. That's why this book was made entirely without the use of exploding staples. You'll get no such promise from *What to Expect When You're Expecting.*

Despite our high standards, we've had to make some compromises to make this book available to the average consumer. For example, our initial plan to surround the sharp edges of each page with six inches of foam padding proved impractical, since it would make every copy of the book roughly fifteen feet thick.

Still, we recognize that some consumers will require a greater level of safety. For them, we are pleased to announce *How Not to Kill Your Baby: Special Edition.* Printed on paper made from organic trees, bound in leather made from vegan cows, the Special Edition represents the state of the art in literary safety. It is available from all quality booksellers for only $49.95.

For an extra $300, you may even purchase an edition written without the use of the letter "e," whose sharp tail could theoretically poke out the eye of a very sensitive child who is looking at the page really, really closely. *How Not to Kill Your Baby: A Form of This Book That Is Not Risky At All on Account of Omitting That Sharp ABC Thing That Follows "D"* is available by special order.

Prenatal Diagnostic Tests

Once upon a time, parents-to-be had to worry that their children would be born with some sort of debilitating condition. But thanks to the wonders of modern science, parents can now spend huge amounts of money on prenatal testing, and then worry that their children will be born with something that the tests didn't catch.

Prenatal tests can be *invasive* (such as a vaginal ultrasound) or *noninvasive* (such as a regular ultrasound, which just involves taking off your shirt and letting a stranger smear jelly on your stomach before sending sound waves into your body to retrieve an image of your unborn child, and, really, what could be invasive about that?)

"So is this the first time you've had a vaginal ultrasound?"

With new tests available every year, it's easy to become overwhelmed. A mother-to-be could take a different test every day of her pregnancy, and still not take them all. That's why it's vital to take at least *two* different tests every day. If your child is going to be afflicted with Shellfish-Triggered Left-handed Albino Narcolepsy, don't you want to know now, so you can begin preparing? Those left-handed oyster-free sunlamps with built-in alarm clocks aren't going to buy themselves.

Staying Fit While Pregnant

It is vital that you maintain a healthy exercise schedule while pregnant. First, this will ensure that you feel fit and healthy, which is useful if you are a selfish monster who puts her own feelings ahead of her child.

More important, you serve as a life support system for your fetus. Your heart pumps blood to your baby; your lungs oxygenate that blood; and your brain prevents you from stumbling into the path of an oncoming train, which could damage your body (or, in medical terms, "the babysack").

FORM OF EXERCISE	SPECIAL PRECAUTIONS NECESSARY WHILE PREGNANT
Running	Make a playlist of upbeat, fast-paced children's songs. Put headphones over your belly.
Football	Buy a little football helmet. Write "Wear this, sweetie!" on it in nontoxic permanent ink. Swallow it.
Cricket	Explain rules of cricket to your fetus. (Note: You must begin this process within minutes of conception, or your baby will be delivered before you finish.)
Yoga	Try not to attain a state of such perfect enlightenment that your consciousness transcends your physical body, as this will later make it difficult to change diapers.

nmm . . . Ommmm . . . Ommmm

MY GOD, STOP KICKING ME! MOMMY IS TRYING TO MEDITATE! . . . Ommmm . . .

DAN'S TIPS FOR DADS-TO-BE

— — — — —

Boy, pregnancy is tough! Even if the wife had the energy for sex, it's kind of hard to reach her you-know-what with a baby in the way! Plus she's always like, "I can't believe you're drinking coffee/boozing it up/smoking a cigar in front of me! That's so thoughtless, Dan!" (Or whatever your own name is—if your wife is calling you by my name, you probably have bigger things to worry about! But maybe your wife should give me a call once she drops the pregnancy weight. Ha ha! Just kidding! Unless you're into that kind of thing, in which case, contact me through the publisher!)

Anyway, it doesn't seem fair that we guys have to put up with all this, but that's the hand Charles Darwin has dealt us. (He invented evolution!) And we have to play it, even if it's got two jokers, and the joker isn't wild but you only put it in the pack because you lost the two of clubs and so you had to write "two of clubs" on one joker in magic marker, and the other guy can read it through the back of the card so he knows what you have. I'm not sure what the second joker represents but I bet it's something bad! Anyway, pregnancy is kind of tough for women, too, so be a sensitive guy and do the right thing: Do all your boozing and smoking at work.

Things You Did Before You
Discovered You Were Pregnant

If you tell your doctor that you drank a glass of wine before you realized you were pregnant, he will tell you, reassuringly, that a single glass of wine is unlikely to do any harm.

However, once you know you're pregnant, your doctor will tell you that no safe level of alcohol consumption during pregnancy has ever been established, and the safest course is not to drink any alcohol at all.

You might conclude that much medical advice about pregnancy is guesswork, and based as much on a desire to avoid lawsuits as on sound scientific research. You would be wrong. The simple fact is that you can do anything you want during pregnancy, *as long as you do not know you are pregnant.* Like Wile E. Coyote as he strolls safely off a cliff, you and your baby are shielded by the remarkable protective powers of ignorance.

The mechanism behind this phenomenon was a mystery for many years, until the recent discovery of a hormone known as "factlackin," which your brain can generate only when it is not busy thinking about something else. By now, it is probably too late for you to avail yourself of this miracle hormone. As soon as this baby is born, though, consider taking the following steps to ensure that you are unaware of any future pregnancies:

- Become morbidly obese.

- Wear only muumuus.

- Sign up to star in the reality show *I Didn't Know I Was Pregnant,* thereby ensuring that your pregnancy ignorance is established contractually.

FOREIGN PREGNANCY

- - - - -

Once you understand the protective powers of ignorance, a whole range of mysteries will be cleared up. For example, if eating pâté is so risky during pregnancy, why are French babies as healthy as any others? If sushi is so dangerous for pregnant women, how have the Japanese endured? Because in French and Japanese, *the word "pregnant" does not exist*. True, a French woman might know she is *enceinte*, while, in more formal Japan, a woman might tell her husband, "*Korega yometara, ura joku ni akusesu shita koto ni narimasu; Gaijin ni wa tagon muyo!*" —but neither woman could know she is *pregnant*, because "pregnant" is an English word, and if it isn't in English, *it simply doesn't count.*

"How amusing! There are two pink lines on this strange stick! Well, off to go smoke some cigarettes while skydiving."

- - - - - - - - -

The Condemned's Last Hours: Preparing for Birth

As your delivery date approaches, you will feel a wealth of conflicting emotions. On the one hand, you will be terrified of the immense responsibility of caring for a newborn child. On the other, you will be terrified of everything that can go wrong during delivery. Then again, you might also feel fear, apprehension, nervousness, and constipation. None of these emotions are cause for worry, unless you begin worrying about worrying about them, or, God forbid, worrying about worrying about worrying, in which case, you might be going insane, and you should begin making preparations to give your child up for adoption.[1]

Otherwise, you will need to make preparations of a different sort. First, of course, you will need to choose a doctor.

---

1   Just make sure your child isn't placed in an orphanage, the home of his nonmagical aunt and uncle, or the river Nile.

Scoping Out Your Medical Professionals

Your obstetrician may assure you that he has a medical degree from Harvard—but which Harvard does he mean? The prestigious medical school in Cambridge, Massachusetts, or the maximum security penitentiary next door? It's a little-known fact, but release forms from the penitentiary look *exactly the same* as degrees from the university. Before subjecting yourself to any prenatal care, demand that all doctors and nurses lift their shirts and allow you to check for prison tattoos.

While you are examining every inch of their skin with a magnifying glass, also look for needle marks. However, keep in mind that not all crippling addictions leave visible signs.

Left to right: heroin; crack cocaine; crystal meth; porn

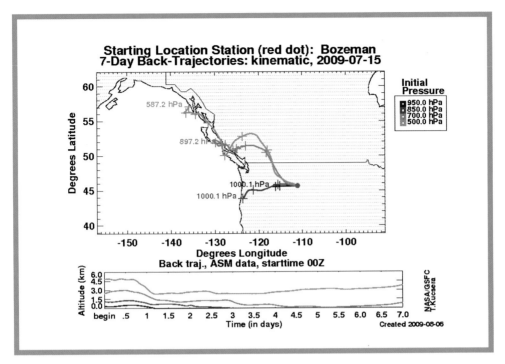

Page 473 of a typical birth plan

Your Birth Plan

A "birth plan" is a document that answers any questions your doctor or midwife might have about your preferences. Do you plan on having an epidural, or would you like to insist on a natural delivery until the pain gets to be too much and you want a fucking epidural RIGHT FUCKING NOW? Do you want a water birth? Would you like to eat the placenta, like Angelina Jolie does, even when the baby's adopted?

Your medical professional will carefully review your birth plan with you and your spouse, asking questions where it is necessary to fully understand your needs and preferences. Then he will ignore them and do whatever he wants. But thanks for all the tips, Ms. I-Didn't-Spend-a-Decade-of-My-Life-Studying-Medicine-but-I-Still-Think-I-Know-Best.

Many hospitals provide portable music devices, allowing you to play songs of your choice during labor. Some parents-to-be simply choose something soothing, but ask yourself this: Do you really want Enrique Iglesias to be the first human voice your baby ever hears?

We recommend you choose music more appropriate to your goals for your child. You might, for example, choose "Hail to the Chief," or the Olympic theme, or, for a more relaxed and folksy approach, a classic country-western hit like "You Can Take My Nobel Prize but Keep Your Cheatin' Hands Off My Dog."

Whichever song you pick, you will then want to loop it endlessly for however long labor takes, lest "Hail to the Chief" not be playing at the precise moment of birth. The only drawback is that this may result in a certain amount of Pavlovian conditioning, causing intense cramping every time you watch a presidential address.

Preparing Your Home

Childproofing

Childproofing your home is easy with this simple seven-step process:

1. Look around your home and identify every single corner—corners can bruise your baby.

2. Cover each corner with soft polyurethane foam.

3. Look around your home and identify every single piece of polyurethane foam—polyurethane polymer dust can cause irritation to your baby's eyes and lungs.

A typical living room before childproofing

A typical living room after childproofing

Or you can just move to the desert, where the rock surfaces have been rubbed smooth by millennia of sandstorms.

4. Cover every polyurethane foam surface with tight-fitting Mylar film.

5. Look around your home and identify every piece of Mylar film—Mylar film is a suffocation risk.

6. Nail wood planking over all Mylar film.

7. Look around your home and identify all wood planking—wood planking has sharp corners, which can bruise your baby.

(Repeat process as necessary.)

Stocking Up

Well before baby comes home, you will want to purchase all of the clothing, toys, books, and other supplies he will need for the next twenty to thirty years. Your friends and family members will be happy to help, by sending you gifts that are just different enough from what you really need to be useless, but just close enough that you'll feel guilty spending money on the thing you actually want.

What you registered for.

What you got.

In deciding which products to purchase, safety must be your primary concern. Unfortunately, it is impossible to childproof toys, since the requisite layers of foam, Mylar, and wood would make them so big and heavy, they would fall on your baby and crush him whenever he tried to play with them.

Instead, you will need to buy products that are safe from the very beginning. And how will you know a product is safe for your baby? It's simple: It will have a picture of a baby on it.

This water is completely safe for your baby.

Every molecule in this bottle contains two atoms of hydrogen— the very same gas that caused the Hindenburg to explode.

Upgrading

When shopping, the sheer variety of options can be overwhelming. Obviously, you will need a solar-powered BPA-free wipe warmer—but *which* solar-powered BPA-free wipe warmer? Don't fret. Simply buy the first one you see. Then, when you see a competing product, use the following chart to determine whether it is better. If so, buy it, too.

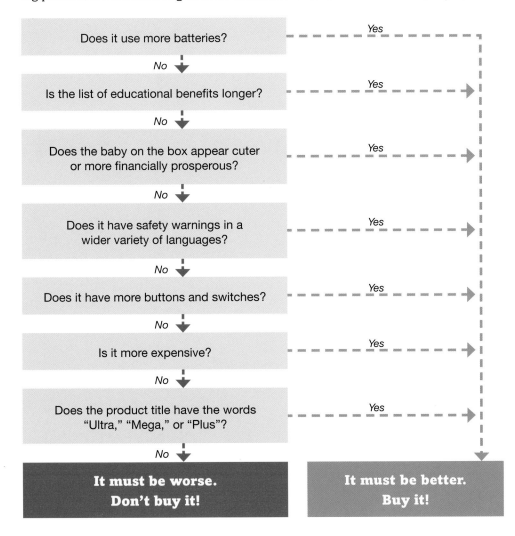

Does it use more batteries? — Yes

No ↓

Is the list of educational benefits longer? — Yes

No ↓

Does the baby on the box appear cuter or more financially prosperous? — Yes

No ↓

Does it have safety warnings in a wider variety of languages? — Yes

No ↓

Does it have more buttons and switches? — Yes

No ↓

Is it more expensive? — Yes

No ↓

Does the product title have the words "Ultra," "Mega," or "Plus"? — Yes

No ↓

It must be worse. Don't buy it!

It must be better. Buy it!

Better Saf-T™ than Sorr-E!

The above advice will eliminate 99 percent of the risks that your baby will face. Thanks to the law of diminishing returns, it would be impossible to eliminate 100 percent of the risks without spending thousands of dollars.

Therefore, you should spend thousands of dollars.

Specifically, you should spend thousands of dollars on the exclusive line of How Not to Kill Your Baby© Saf-T Produx™. Compare a can of patented How Not to Kill Your Baby© Saf-T Brand™ Infant Formula with Brand X. Just by glancing at the labels, you can tell that How Not to Kill Your Baby© Saf-T Brand™ Infant Formula is much better.

And the improvements don't stop there!

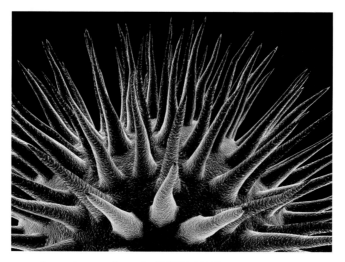

On a microscopic scale, EVERYTHING has sharp edges.

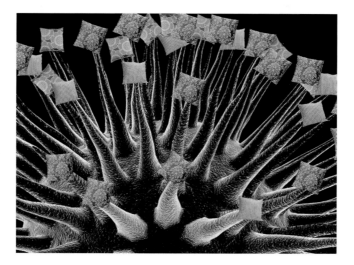

All How Not to Kill Your Baby© Saf-T Produx™ are coated with billions of nano-pillows, to make sure your baby is protected right down to the microscopic level!

Although her parents gave her a normal American first name, Suzie Slutzky was pretty much doomed from birth.

Choosing a Name

If at all possible, try to choose your baby's name in advance; parents who wait until after birth are frequently too exhausted by labor to make a sensible decision.

Left to right: Whatever Peng; Don'tBotherMeIJustWantAFrickinShower Jones; and Asadkljhrw3rw Greenblatt-Gutierrez

Every culture has its own method of naming children. In some, children are named in honor of living relatives. In many Jewish families, by contrast, children are named only in honor of *deceased* relatives. If you are Jewish, and a living relative of yours has a name you particularly like, you may need to encourage them to take up skydiving or shark wrestling. Indeed, it is a little known fact that Murder, Inc.—a famed group of Jewish hit men from the 1930s—was initially formed for the express purpose of freeing up popular first names.

Remember, though: The most important thing when picking a name is not honoring your cultural heritage or creating a link between the generations. It is avoiding playground bullying. Before you pick a name, ask yourself, "Does this name sound like, look like, or abbreviate to anything remotely unflattering?" If the answer is "Yes," you will need to find a new name for your child.

NAME	POSSIBLE PLAYGROUND INSULT
Harry	None, unless your last name is "Johnson" or "Wang."
John	"John means toilet! Poopy John! Poopy John!"
Mary	"Although Mary sometimes refers to the Virgin Mary, it can also describe Mary Magdalene, a fallen woman! Hey, Mary, why don't you go commit some sins of the flesh?"
Richard	"Dick! Dicky dick dick dick!"
Farty Farthead	"Arty Arthead."

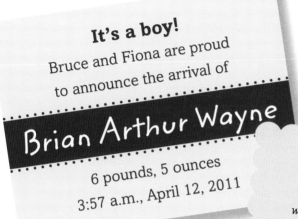

It's a boy!

Bruce and Fiona are proud to announce the arrival of

Brian Arthur Wayne

6 pounds, 5 ounces
3:57 a.m., April 12, 2011

IT'S A GIRL!

Charles and Beverly Wilson,

whose annual income is so low as to make kidnapping their daughter highly unprofitable,

are pleased to take a break from their kickboxing and riflery classes to welcome

Chloé Julia Wilson

5 pounds, 9 ounces
2:30 a.m., April 12, 2011

(At which time their home, though seemingly empty, was guarded by two Doberman pinschers, as it always is. Not that they have anything worth stealing. In fact, they can barely afford to even feed the dogs, so they're always really hungry.)

Writing the Birth Announcement

Many parents prefer to write the birth announcement before the child is born, and then fill in the details later. Few parents, however, realize that the announcement itself can be a source of danger to your child. Here are two sample announcements. Can you tell which one was written by parents who have taken proper precautions?

With the due date long past and no sign of labor, the twins decided to make themselves comfortable inside Marge's womb.

CHAPTER 4

Push Harder, Damn It! The Miracle of Birth

As you enter the ninth month, you will find yourself more and more ready to give birth. If you find yourself in the tenth or eleventh month, you may be even more eager. Don't worry, though! Missing your due date is just nature's way of telling you that you're entirely unprepared for parenthood and you've made a terrible mistake. (Giving birth *before* your due date, by contrast, simply shows that you lack the patience to be a good parent, and you've made a terrible mistake.)

*"I don't know what this does, Honey,
but we'd better pack it just to be safe."*

Packing Your Bags

Well before you head to the hospital, make sure you have everything you'll need for a smooth delivery:

- A toothbrush and other overnight essentials

- Baby's first outfit

- Baby's second outfit, after baby spits up over baby's first outfit

- Baby's third through fortieth outfits

DAN'S TIPS FOR DADS-TO-BE

— — — — —

Buddy, right about now, your wife is going to feel like the Goodyear Blimp. And she's going to look like it, too. But don't tell her that! Because women—well, gosh, they can be awful sensitive! Instead, try finding something positive to say. Like, "You must have a great view of the playing field from up there!"

- Grappling hooks and rope to fasten yourself to the ground, in case a tornado pulls off the roof of the hospital

- Suntan lotion, in case the roof-destroying tornado is immediately followed by blazing sunshine

- Shark repellant, in case the sharks who have been plucked out of the ocean and dropped in the hospital parking lot by the tornado flee inside to escape the blazing sun

- Snacks

Arranging for Help

Gone are the days when a pregnant mother arrived at the hospital with only her husband. Today's couples have a wide range of professionals available to assist them:

- A *doula* will offer you nonmedical support by giving you massages, keeping you hydrated, and helping you maintain a positive attitude.

- A *birth coach* is similar to a doula, but if your attitude isn't positive enough, he will order you to drop and give him twenty.

- A *hypnotherapist* will help ease the pain of delivery without using anesthesia.

Can't afford a hypnotherapist? Don't worry! Simply cut out these pictures and tape them to the insides of your eyelids.

- A *malpractice attorney* will sue the doula, the birth coach, and the hypnotherapist when they crash into the doctor while jostling for position between your legs, sending your baby flying like a football.

Your baby's first glimpse of the world

Labor: An Hour-by-Hour Guide

Two Weeks to Two Hours Before Labor

Lightening occurs when the baby sinks lower into your pelvis. If the baby's position has caused you discomfort in the previous months of pregnancy, lightening will grant you some relief, by causing you to feel an entirely different discomfort. The *bloody show* refers to the expulsion of the mucous sealing the cervix, unless you are Michael Caine, in which case it refers to any program on television.

Braxton Hicks contractions can leave a woman wondering if labor has begun, but they are actually fairly easy to distinguish from real contractions. Simply wait ten years, then check the birthday of your ten-year-old child.

Labor Begins

The *first stage* of labor is broken up into three parts, because it's just too much fun to restrict to one.

1. During the *early labor phase*, you will feel mild contractions and your water may break, especially if you have just sat down on an irreplaceable piece of antique furniture. During this stage, distract yourself with simple, relaxing activities, like assembling a crib from five pieces of particle board and three thousand nuts and bolts, all of which look identical but won't fit unless you have found exactly the right one. Also, try breathing.

2. During the *active labor phase*, your contractions will be stronger and closer together. Now is the time to head to the hospital. If you have chosen a home birth, you should nonetheless run out of your house, frantically hail a cab, and ask to be driven around the block a dozen times as quickly as possible, just so you don't deprive yourself of the traditional "race to the hospital" suspense.

ALTERNATIVE VIEWS OF LABOR

— — — — —

In recent years, alternative perspectives on labor have begun to spring up. Whether arguing for water birth, home birth, or some other possibility, advocates of these new viewpoints say that delivering a baby does not have to be quite as painful as is widely supposed. Indeed, they argue that the very fear of pain may *cause* more pain, since tension causes muscles to tighten, including the vaginal muscles through which the baby must pass. Although they acknowledge that some discomfort is inevitable, they claim that the endless focus on the horrors of childbirth is at best misguided, and at worst the sign of an industry built around terrorizing pregnant women and new parents for profit.

DO NOT LISTEN TO THESE PEOPLE! THEY WANT TO KILL YOUR BABY! THEN THEY WANT TO EAT IT! Also, they are IN YOUR BASEMENT RIGHT NOW! If you don't have a basement, THEY ARE BUILDING ONE UNDER YOUR FEET AT THIS VERY MOMENT, JUST SO THEY HAVE SOMEPLACE TO HIDE!

THE ONLY WAY TO SAVE YOUR BABY IS TO ORDER THE $499.95 HOW NOT TO KILL YOUR BABY™ SAYF-TEA© BASEMENT SHIELD, AVAILABLE NOW IN HOSPITAL GIFT SHOPS AND BABY SUPPLY STORES EVERYWHERE.

3. During the *transition phase,* contractions will be extremely strong and intense, and by the end of it, your cervix will have dilated to about ten centimeters. You might imagine that such a large dilation would be enough for a newborn to pass easily through. Ha ha ha ha ha ha ha! Boy, are you in for a surprise!

Labor, Part II: The Baby's Revenge

The *second stage* of labor often begins with a period of relative calm. Take a few moments to rest for the efforts ahead, because there's nothing like ten seconds of deep breathing to get you ready for two hours of squeezing an entire human being out of the most sensitive part of your body.

Then it will be time for you to push. There are countless different positions for pushing. For best results, you should use the same position you used for conception, but if the hospital does not have a mud pit, a motorcycle, and a quarter-scale model of the U.S. House of Representatives, you may need to consider alternatives. Look at the positions on the opposite page, and choose whichever one feels most comfortable and natural.

Whatever position you choose, be sure to thank your doctor, midwife, spouse, or other birthing coach for reminding you to push, because with a human being wedged into your vaginal canal, and every muscle in your body squeezing rhythmically like a python devouring a Great Dane, and a million years of evolutionary instinct telling you what to do, it couldn't possibly have occurred to you to push if somebody who might not have a vaginal canal and certainly doesn't have a person in it wasn't yelling helpful advice right into your face.

At the appropriate point, be sure to ask to have a mirror positioned so that you can see your baby begin to emerge. Also be sure to ask for a blindfold so that you don't have to see your baby begin to emerge.

Leaning on birth ball

Birthing ball squeezed in hand (Note: Only suitable if you are eighty feet tall)

The Standing Fliederholtz

The Inverse Retton (Note: Only to be used with a trapeze-mounted midwife)

The Triple Lindy (suitable for multiple births)

The Moments After Birth

Finally, after nine months of pregnancy and five thousand hours of labor, the moment will arrive. You will, at last, meet your baby. As you know if you have ever seen someone give birth in a movie or television show, all newborns emerge with adorable round faces, pudgy limbs, and twinkling eyes.

If, by contrast, the nurse hands you a tiny, squawling creature with the face of an old man and skin covered in goo, hand it back immediately. There has clearly been some sort of mix-up with a nearby ward for senile midgets.

If the birth was particularly difficult, your smiling, rosy-cheeked baby may arrive in slightly wrinkled clothes.

The Apgar Test

The Apgar test is a simple ten-point test used to determine the health of a newborn. Your obstetrician will administer it one minute after your baby is born, which gives you exactly sixty seconds to help her cram. Unfortunately, many newborns seem unaware of the importance of high test scores, so you may have a hard time getting your ten-second-old infant to focus on the flash cards.

Don't give up! And don't be afraid to ask the doctor for more time. If he insists that the test has to be taken *right now*, it's probably just because he has his own newborn and he doesn't want your child one day competing for space at a highly competitive kindergarten.

APGAR RANGE	FUTURE POSITION
10	President of the United States
9	United States senator
8	Member of the House of Representatives
7	Governor of a highly populous state
6	Governor of Rhode Island
5	Mayor of a major metropolitan area
4	Small-town sheriff
3	State senator
2	Garbage collector
1	Vice president of the United States

"The good news is, your baby has two perfectly formed hands. The bad news is, one of them is freakishly large."

The First Poop

For a few days after birth, your baby will pass *meconium*, his first poops. This will be a thick, tarry, sticky substance that looks like something BP would leak into the Gulf of Mexico, and which will prove just as difficult to clean. Meconium can also be found in specialty stores under the name "Vegemite."

Because meconium contains traces of any substances ingested by the fetus during pregnancy, it is sometimes tested for alcohol or narcotics, and meconium samples can be turned over to child protective services for further examination. The lesson is clear: Whatever you do, never work for child protective services.

ATTACH
BABY HERE

- - - - - - - - -

CHAPTER 5

The First, and
Quite Possibly Last, Days

H ere's a simple quiz to see whether you are fit to be a parent. Just read the following statement and decide whether it is true or false. And don't feel the need to rush—you have all the time in the world.[1]

From the moment you first bring your newborn child into your home, safety will be your primary concern. TRUE FALSE

If you answered "True," then you have already failed as a parent. Please return this book to the vendor, after first gluing your baby's elbow to the space provided.

---

1   Unless your child has already been born, in which case, while you linger leisurely over this quiz, he is exploring an electrical socket with a sharp knife.

Those of you who answered the quiz correctly know that safety must begin *before* you bring your child into your home. On the drive from the hospital, it is absolutely essential that your child is properly strapped into a car seat. Fortunately, this is a simple process, as the diagram on the next page indicates.

If it looks a little confusing, don't worry. You and your spouse will find it much easier when one of you is holding a crying, helpless infant, and the other is experiencing a primeval adrenalin rush that would have been useful to your distant ancestors when protecting their offspring from mastodons, but in your case, the only effect is to make your hands shake frantically while you attempt to install a complicated piece of equipment. Oh, and did we mention that if you do it wrong, your child will die?

DAN'S TIPS FOR DADS

— — — — —

Once they've gotten the kid home, a lot of dads feel about as useful as a bowling pin on a football field—during the off-season! And that's not very useful!

But the fact is, there are *tons* of things you can do to help your wife out with a newborn. For example, there's . . .

Um . . .

Huh.

Let me get back to you on this one!

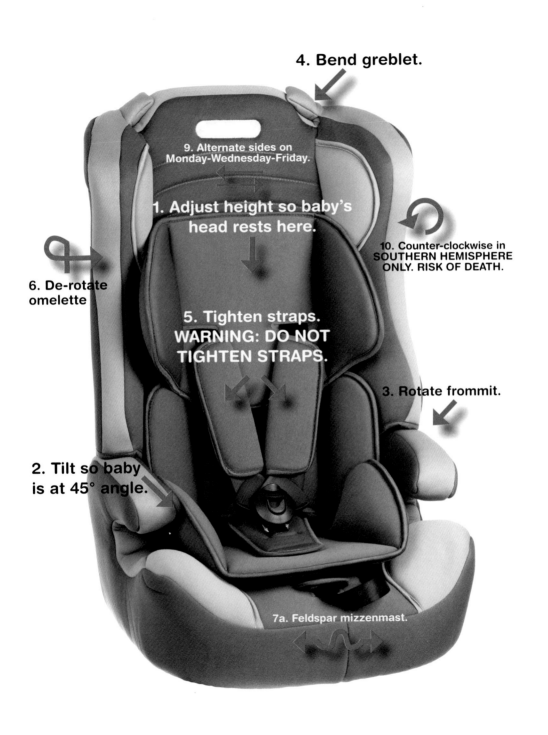

4. Bend greblet.

9. Alternate sides on Monday-Wednesday-Friday.

1. Adjust height so baby's head rests here.

10. Counter-clockwise in SOUTHERN HEMISPHERE ONLY. RISK OF DEATH.

6. De-rotate omelette

5. Tighten straps. WARNING: DO NOT TIGHTEN STRAPS.

3. Rotate frommit.

2. Tilt so baby is at 45° angle.

7a. Feldspar mizzenmast.

Alternate Methods of Transportation

Don't own a car? Don't worry! There are as many ways of bringing a baby home from the hospital as there are loser unemployed parents who can't afford their own automobile. But before taking advantage of any of them, make sure to consult the following table.

METHOD OF TRANSPORTATION	RISK TO BABY	SUITABLE PRECAUTION
Walking home, with baby in stroller	Being run over by someone successful enough to own a car	Walk with groveling posture to avoid provoking the ire of your betters.
Dogsled	Dog bites	Have sled pulled by bunnies.
Horseback	Being held up by outlaws over by the dry gulch	Nine months before delivery, sleep with white-hat-wearing masked crusader for justice, conceiving baby with uncanny quick-draw skills.
Public transportation	Exposure to people who support public transportation, which is one step away from socialism, which is one step away from snatching babies from their parents and putting them in state-run collective orphanages	Vote Republican.

Breast-feeding

Breast-feeding is one of the most natural things a woman can do. For hundreds of thousands of years, it has been an instinctive bond between mother and child—an unending dance of nurture and love. Untold millennia ago, in a fire-lit cavern in a prehistoric jungle, your ancient ancestor knew exactly how to nourish her fragile newborn. You, however, are doing it all wrong.

Effective breast-feeding begins with proper infant positioning. Refer to the following diagram for help.

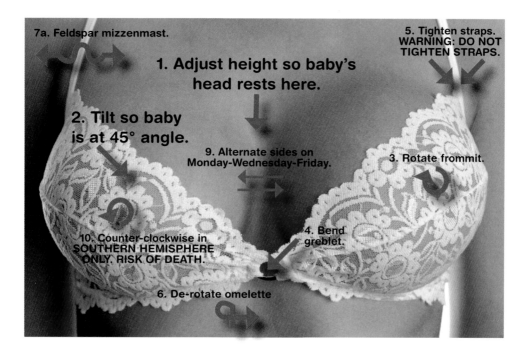

7a. Feldspar mizzenmast.

5. Tighten straps. WARNING: DO NOT TIGHTEN STRAPS.

1. Adjust height so baby's head rests here.

2. Tilt so baby is at 45° angle.

9. Alternate sides on Monday-Wednesday-Friday.

3. Rotate frommit.

10. Counter-clockwise in SOUTHERN HEMISPHERE ONLY. RISK OF DEATH.

4. Bend greblet.

6. De-rotate omelette

Once you have mastered the art of attaching a crying, wriggling infant to a tiny target at precisely the right angle, the hard work can begin. Make sure to be conscious of the following advice at all times while breast-feeding. You may wish to write it on your baby's scalp with a magic marker, just to have it handy.

- Relaxation is vital. Begin by putting from your mind all stressful thoughts, such as the myriad deadly risks your baby will face, or the medical costs associated with delivery, or future expenses like college, for which you almost certainly haven't saved enough. Also, try not to worry about global warming. And bee stings. Definitely don't think about those. Unfortunately, merely by reading this paragraph, you have created an indelible mental linkage between breast-feeding and bee stings; if possible, try not to have read this paragraph.

DO NOT LOOK AT THE ABOVE PHOTO
UNDER ANY CIRCUMSTANCES.

The last thing Clarissa remembered was feeding Marlon three times from the same breast, then going to bed.

- If your baby begins one nursing session on the left breast, make sure he begins the next one on the right. Otherwise, one breast could balloon into a room-filling gigantazoid. To prevent this from happening, put a safety pin on the outside of your shirt to indicate which breast you last nursed from. *Important note*: Do not let the pin prick your one humongous breast, lest it explode in a massive, room-destroying eruption of milk.

- Finally, please keep in mind that this ancient and beautiful display of unconditional maternal love is totally gross, and nobody wants to see you do it. You may be cursed with the rare two-week-old who is simply too greedy to stick with three meals a day at regularly predictable times, forcing you to occasionally breast-feed in public. If so, you may wish to cover your exposed breasts with a How Not to Kill Your Baby™ Sayy-f-T Brand Vinyl Shame Cover, decorated with a handsome painting of a more societally acceptable image, such as a man adjusting his balls.

DAN'S TIPS FOR DADS

— — — — —

I've figured it out. The one essential thing that a new dad can do to help with a newborn is . . .

No, wait. Now that I think about it, that one really isn't very necessary at all. Sorry. Come back to me in a few minutes. I'll definitely have something!

A WORD TO NEW MOTHERS

Focused as you are on taking care of your child, you may not be devoting sufficient time to taking care of yourself. But the past nine months have been hard on you, and you have earned every right to a little relaxation. Give yourself a break. Take some time to put your feet up, drink some herbal tea, and read a favorite book or magazine. And don't be stingy—stretch your "me time" out to ten, or even fifteen, seconds. You deserve every one of them.

A typical picture before labor

During this extended period of rest, you may notice that your body looks somewhat different than it did before labor. Oh, your belly will still be huge, even though it's no longer holding a baby. So don't worry—you won't need to buy skinnier jeans for many months, or, more likely, ever. That's just one of the many ways in which motherhood will help save you money! The physical aftereffects of delivery include hair loss from hormonal changes; black eyes, as well as bruising all over the body, from the strain of pushing; and an aching or even fractured tailbone. If you don't have all or most of these symptoms, then you didn't try hard enough during labor. Go back to the maternity ward and ask if you can try again.

A typical picture after

Swaddling

The months immediately after birth are often referred to as "the fourth trimester." After nine months of pregnancy, there is still developmental work to be done, but if the fetus stayed in the womb any longer, its ever-growing head would not fit through the mother's pelvis. In that sense, all children, no matter how long they are carried, are expelled prematurely from the womb. In other words, among the things setting you up for failure as a parent is *the very phenomenon of evolution itself.*

Until women evolve the thigh muscles necessary to keep their legs crossed really, really tightly for an extra three months,

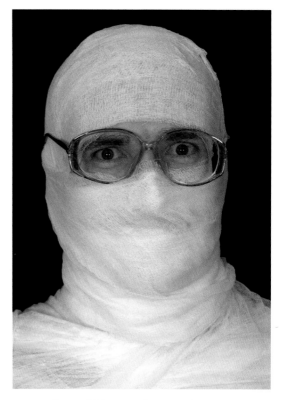

Some children continue to enjoy being swaddled well into the ninety-sixth trimester.

you can help re-create the warm, cozy feeling of the uterus by swaddling your baby.[2]

Swaddling involves wrapping an unhappy wriggling baby in a narrow piece of cloth. In addition to making your baby feel more secure, it has the advantage of making child safety seat installation seem relatively simple.

---

2   You can help the rest of us by not using the words "warm and cozy" to refer to your uterus, because, honestly, there's something a little creepy about it.

How your baby sees you

A Baby's Developing Visual System

Don't worry if your baby doesn't pay attention to the expensive mobile you've hung above his crib. Most likely, it's just a sign that the mobile isn't expensive *enough*. Try exchanging it for one covered in gold and precious stones.

If that still doesn't work, it's probably because your baby's visual system is still developing. To a one-week-old, anything more than a foot away will be blurry, and only the highest contrast black-and-white images will catch his attention. In other words, to your baby, the warm and colorful nursery you've painstakingly designed looks like a still from a 1920s German horror film.

Sex

Once upon a time, medical professionals recommended waiting as much as six weeks after delivery before recommencing sexual relations. Now, however, doctors feel that, in most cases of normal delivery, there is no need to have sex ever again. After all, you've already successfully reproduced. What more do you want? Some sort of selfish, hedonistic physical pleasure? *With your innocent baby in the very same house?* You ought to be ashamed of yourself.

CHAPTER 6

The First, and Almost Certainly Last, Months

By the time your baby is a few weeks old, you are a much more experienced parent. You change diapers one-handedly and you burp your baby confidently. You may even shower weekly.

As a result, you may find yourself losing touch with the jumpy, fearful new parent you once were. *You must not allow this to happen.* It is your fear that keeps the baby alive. Imagine, for a moment, that you are in a primeval jungle, millennia ago. Do you know what would happen the instant you relaxed? *A cave bear would eat your baby.* Not so proud of that one-handed diaper-changing thing now, are you?

Now imagine that you are in an elevator holding your baby, and the cable is suddenly cut, sending you both plunging downward. Also imagine that the elevator is full of scorpions. Plus, you owe the scorpions money. Implant this image in your heart and reflect on it anytime you are tempted to enjoy parenthood.

If that doesn't do the trick, you can also just read the rest of this chapter.

Warning Signs

Many babies are perfectly healthy—perhaps as many as two or three of them. However, it is important to look out for warning signs that may reflect serious mental or physical problems.

SYMPTOM	MOST LIKELY CAUSE
Drooling	Baby is a cannibal and is fantasizing about eating you.
Inability to walk	In preparation for robbing your house, baby is carefully establishing an alibi, because how could he climb in that second-story window if he can't even walk? Huh? Answer that, copper. You'll never pin anything on baby! Baby is in the clear!
Frequent crying	Bad parenting. (Note: This is also a likely explanation for everything else your child will do for the next seventy years.)
Doesn't poop for several hours, then as soon as you remove the diaper, lets forth a massive brown stream all over your arm	Baby is not a cannibal, but many of his friends are, and he is trying to save your life by making you as unappetizing as possible.
Falls asleep frequently	Baby is insufficiently stressed. Read him this chapter immediately.

Taking Baby Outside

Most of the time, you'll want to keep your baby safely inside, in a temperature- and humidity-controlled room with black windows (to filter out ultraviolet light, which can cause cancer) and sunlight-replicating lamps (to provide ultraviolet light, which your baby needs to generate vitamin D).

Sometimes, though, you'll have no choice but to leave your house. Perhaps you will need to take your baby to one of his hourly medical checkups, or perhaps your home is about to be hit by a comet. Either way, you'll want to make sure you're prepared for all the hazards of the outside world.

First, strip your baby naked and apply sunscreen to every crevice of his body, even the ones that will be completely covered, and even if you are only going out at night. Sunlight is a wily foe, and your baby must be shielded from it at all costs.[1]

Now, make sure your baby has a hat. If it's cold, choose a warm woolen hat. If it's hot, choose a warm woolen hat that you've kept in the freezer. If you're going to a formal event, or if you are Father Time and your baby is the physical incarnation of the New Year, choose a jaunty top hat. Whatever the situation, the simple fact is that babies need hats. If you don't believe it, try taking your baby outside without one. Suddenly, you will find yourself surrounded by dozens of grandmothers, nipping at you. Oh, you can point out to them that it's a hundred degrees, plus your particular baby hates hats and squirms out of any one you put on, and, in fact, thanks to a rare genetic condition, he doesn't even have a head, but they won't care. Why? BECAUSE BABIES NEED HATS.

Also, give your baby some clothes.

---

1   *Important note:* This recommendation is based on medical advice at the time of publication. If you are reading this book sometime after 2020, when sunscreen will turn out to be a deadly carcinogen, please replace this paragraph with the following: "Next, carefully remove any traces of sunscreen from every crevice of your baby's body. Sunscreen is a wily foe, and your baby must be shielded from it at all costs."

Finally encase your baby in an oxygenated plastic bubble, which you will coat with gamma-ray-filtering micro paint, and then mount on armored, land-mine-resistant treads equipped with front- and side-facing air bags. Then put another hat on top of the bubble, just to be safe.

Or you can just use UPS.

Breast-feeding Revisited

By the start of the second month, some mothers are still having a difficult time breast-feeding. Specifically, you are. Everybody else has it down perfectly.

But don't worry. Experts currently recommend that children be breast-fed for the first twelve years, which gives you plenty of time to get it right.

DAN'S TIPS FOR DADS

Hi, dads! If your special lady is still having a hard time breast-feeding, you might want to try a little trick called the "Play-by-Play." Just pretend her nipple is the forty-yard line and you're Jimmy Johnson! It might go a little something like this:

"Good job, honey! He just latched on. Oops, he slipped off. Try lifting up your elbow a little—no, the left elbow. That's right! He latched on again! Oops, he slipped off again! What if you use a pillow?"

Trust me—she'll love it! Also, try following her into the toilet sometimes, because this technique works great if she's constipated, too!

Sleep

Experts advise that babies should be sleeping through the night by the age of three months. Experts also define "sleeping through the night" as sleeping for a single five-hour stretch sometime after dark.

If your baby is not reaching this milestone, you may want to try giving your baby a light snack before bedtime. (Experts define "a light snack" as an uninterrupted eighteen-hour feed.) You might also try switching to a slightly co-zier crib. (Experts define "a slightly co-zier crib" as a custom-built, form-fitted baby chamber composed of sustainably sourced hardwood shaped to be precisely 1.3 inches away from the surface of your baby's skin at every point.)

The Wibberleys finally found a use for all those books by sleep experts.

Keeping Good Records

It's essential that you keep careful track of your baby's every bodily function. That way, when she is president of the United States, and a paranoid-minded conspiracy movement springs up denying her eligibility for the position, you will have documentary proof that she did, in fact, poop on U.S. soil at 8:23 a.m. on February 23.

Here is what a simple record of your baby's day might look like:

Y A W N S	B U R P S
9:45 a.m.	8 a.m.
9:51 a.m.	1:03 p.m.
12:34 p.m.	(? Not sure of time—forgot to write it down until two minutes later. Could have been 1:02 p.m. or even 1:01 p.m.)
6:15 p.m.	

S N E E Z E S	A D O R A B L E L I T T L E H I C C U P S
4:00 a.m.	Steadily, from 1:46 p.m. to 6:29 p.m.

POOP

TIME	VOLUME
3:55 a.m.	45.677 ml
5:20 a.m.	12.0234 ml
3:01 p.m.	123 ml exactly

PEE

TIME	VOLUME
12 noon	45 ml
1:47 p.m.	30 ml
2:39 p.m.	100 ml
3:42 p.m.	80 ml
4:10 p.m.	35 ml
5:32 p.m.	5 liters

A R O M A

Woodsy

Oaky, with a pungent aftertaste of buttercup and well water, culminating in a rush of tannins.

Poopy

W H E R E   P E E   E N D E D   U P

Diaper

Diaper

Daddy's eyes

Father O'Malley's sleeve

Diaper

Mommy's nose; Daddy's sweater; Persian rug; dog's fur; bathtub; telephone; sink; ceiling; staircase; next-door neighbor's bed (window was open!); antique print of New Bedford, Massachusetts, whaling scene.

NAP START	NAP END
10:00 a.m.	10:15 a.m.
11:20 a.m.	11:21 a.m.
1:05 p.m.	1:45 p.m.
6:30 p.m.	10:00 p.m.
10:05 p.m.	4:00 a.m.
4:15 a.m.	6:00 a.m.
6:00 a.m.	7:30 a.m.

SLEEP

NURSING START	NURSING END
12:01 a.m.	11:59 p.m.

NURSING

WHAT YOU HAD TO DO TO GET HIM TO SLEEP

Rock gently while shushing

Rock gently while shushing and bouncing on the soles of feet

Rock gently while shushing and bouncing on the soles of feet, then swaying hips like Elvis

Rock gently while shushing and bouncing on soles of feet, then swaying hips like Elvis, then singing "Rock-a-Bye Baby" eighteen times, then swaying hips more, then bouncing more, then singing "Rock-a-Bye Baby" twice more before giving up and turning on evening news, at which point baby fell asleep the instant Brian Williams started talking

Played recording of Brian Williams

Played recording of Brian Williams

Played recording of Brian Williams

WHICH BREAST

left

Returning to Work

For many women, returning to work is nearly as difficult a transition as becoming a mother—an endless series of missed moments that can never be recovered, all the while balancing the mutually exclusive roles of nurturing, ever-present life giver and career-minded twenty-first-century feminist. Many men also find it difficult, because they have to spend a few extra minutes dabbing spit-up off their suits.

Here are some tips to make the transition easier:

- Simulate the parenting experience by working for a boss who yells at you constantly, changes his mind every few minutes, and expects you to clean up his messes.

- Take a job that allows you to work at night, then spend all day with your baby. (This will require outsourcing your sleep needs to an inexpensive nap surrogate in India.)

- Consider taking your baby to work with you. If this is against company policy, dress him up in a suit and tie and tell everybody that he is "Ernesto Grzbclik," a very short new hire from a country whose language consists of extended crying.

Betsy's plan backfired when Joey got promoted to a management position, then put her on probation for "insufficient Pixie Stick purchases."

CHAPTER 7

Months Six Through Twelve, Unless You Have Already Killed Your Baby, in Which Case You Can Stop Reading Now

T he first six months can feel like an endless marathon, so congratulations! You've made it halfway through your baby's first year. Just twenty and a half years left to go![1]

First Words

On the average, children speak their first word sometime around their first birthday. If you don't want your child to be average, therefore, you'll need to start teaching him to talk at roughly six months. Here are some techniques you might use:

---

[1] Assuming they don't major in English and move back in with you after college.

- Never speak to your baby. Eventually, the extended conversational pause will be so awkward, he'll feel compelled to break the silence.

- Alternatively, read to your baby every day, twenty-four hours a day. Pause only to point to people who aren't reading and say, "See that jerk? He's not reading. What a loser!"

- Fill your baby's mouth full of marbles, which you vaguely remember was kind of like something some famous Greek once did or something. (Note: To avoid choking hazard, marbles should be bowling-ball-sized.)

- Learn ventriloquism.

Baby Sign Language

Control over the fine muscles of the mouth and larynx is more complicated than control over fingers and hands, and develops much later. As a result, even children who cannot yet speak are able to communicate using sign language.

Teaching your child sign language has several advantages. It allows them to express themselves at a young age, helping to prevent tantrums. It lets them develop the mental skills that will ultimately make spoken language possible. It offers a vital safety precaution in case they are pursued by kidnappers and the only police officers around are deaf. But, most important, *it allows you to win.* (See next page.)

Words spoken by sign language still count as words, which means your child's first words can come that much earlier than everybody else's. (Unfortunately, scientists have not yet developed sign potty training, but they're working on it.)

Maggie learned all her baby signs from watching Monday Night Football.

THE THRILL OF VICTORY, THE AGONY OF NOT HAVING ANY TEETH AFTER A WHOLE YEAR OF CHECKING THOSE LITTLE PINK GUMS

— — — — —

Many baby books offer lists of milestones that babies might reach at a given age. We have resisted the urge to do so, because all babies develop differently. What is important is not whether your child has grown his first tooth at five months old or said his first word at eight months. What is important is that he is doing those things faster than other children, because that means you win.

Some books will urge you not to feel like your child is competing with other children. Those books are written by losers.

Other books will acknowledge that competitive feelings are inevitable, but they will counsel you not to let those feelings drive your approach to parenting; you must not (they will continue) pressure your children to progress faster than their natural pace. These books are not written by losers. They are written by clever people who want *your* children to lose, because that means less competition for their own children.

Rest assured: All books in the How Not to Kill Your Baby™ series are written by people who not only don't have children, but have never actually interacted with them. How Not to Kill Your Baby™: a name you can trust!

Translating Baby's First Words

Hearing your baby's first halting speech will be a deeply emotional moment; no matter how much you feel you have learned about them during their short time on Earth, their first words will give you a once-in-a-lifetime opportunity to discover something new and horrible about them.

FIRST WORD	HORRIBLE THING IT REVEALS
"Mama"	Baby has formed an unnatural attachment to his or her mother.
"Dada"	Baby has formed an unnatural attachment to either his father or the surrealist movement championed by Salvador Dalí.
"Cat"	Baby is destined to grow up into one of those old women with dozens of cats. (This is true whether baby is a boy or a girl.)
"Uh-oh"	Baby is already aware of your numerous parenting mistakes.
"Cheese"	Baby is already aware of your numerous parenting mistakes and is practicing to have his picture taken for an adoption brochure.

Minimum protection for a walking-age baby

Best protection

First Steps

Most children take their first steps at around twelve months of age, but some begin walking as early as nine months. As a precaution, starting around six months, your baby should begin wearing a helmet twenty-four hours a day.

Sleep-Training Techniques

If your baby is still not sleeping through the night by the time she is six months old, you may need to try sleep training by one of the following methods.

- *Crying it out* involves putting your baby in his crib, closing the nursery door, and not opening it until morning. When you do return, you will either have a happy and self-confident baby who has learned to sleep

When the Gundersons finally worked out a way to get Henry to sleep, it involved gravity boots and a tight grip.

through the night or a psychologically damaged future terrorist who will never sleep again. (On the plus side, a nocturnal schedule is a significant career advantage for terrorists, so your baby benefits either way.)

- *Ferberizing* is a variation on crying it out, but parents return to the room at steadily growing intervals to reassure the baby. Although it can take longer to work than crying it out, Ferberizing is less stressful for parent and child, and when it goes seriously wrong, at least it produces terrorists who call home on the way to the airport.

- *Co-sleeping* is the practice of bringing your baby into bed with you. The advantage is that babies sleep better when they have a larger family member to snuggle up with. The disadvantage is that parents frequently sleep much more poorly, but this can be remedied by making sure that both parents have even larger family members to snuggle up to, such as a morbidly obese uncle.

  At some point, your children will need to be weaned off co-sleeping. This is most commonly done by sending them off to college, where they can begin co-sleeping with people their own age.

THE FIVE STAGES OF SLEEP DEPRIVATION

— — — — — —

Experts have identified five stages of sleep deprivation in parents:

Stage 1: Although it would not be apparent to a casual observer, you are operating at slightly less than peak efficiency.

Stage 2: You stumble over words and appear bleary-eyed.

Stage 3: It is unsafe for you to operate a motor vehicle.

Stage 4: It is unsafe for you to operate an electric toothbrush.

Stage 5: It is unsafe for your child to visit The Hague, because the level of sleep deprivation he has subjected you to will result in prosecution under the Geneva Conventions.

Occasionally, you will encounter other parents who will assure you that you will never again get enough sleep. They will chuckle and look proud of themselves, as if they've just said something funny. These are people who once progressed to the legendary Stage 6, spoken about only in terrified whispers, and it has permanently damaged their brains. Rest assured: One day, you *will* get eight hours of uninterrupted sleep.

Then you will wake up to discover the entire nursery was carried away in a flood.

DAN'S TIPS FOR DADS

— — — — —

Guys, if your wife has suggested co-sleeping, I know exactly what your reaction was! You gave a long speech about how important it was to promote independent sleep habits but inside you were thinking "OH NO, PLEASE GOD I WOULD ONE DAY LIKE TO HAVE SEX AGAIN!"

Well, don't worry, this is actually going to work out great. Just tell your wife you really value the "emotional connection" of "physical intimacy" and you'd hate to lose that "soul-to-soul contact." (Try to keep a straight face!) She'll tell you not to worry, because co-sleeping advocates suggest having "intimacy" in places other than the bed.

That's right: Your wife just agreed to some hot and nasty kitchen table intimacy! Shut the curtains and roll up the rugs, cause you're about to get intimate on the floor and you don't want your knees getting burned! Get on Facebook and start looking up willing exes, because it's time for some hot girl-on-girl intimacy! (That might be pushing your luck. But the kitchen table thing is still pretty boss!)

Attachment Parenting

Co-sleeping is an important part of a philosophy known as "attachment parenting." Advocates of attachment parenting believe that the mother should breast-feed the baby on demand, carry the baby whenever possible, sleep with the baby, and respond immediately whenever the baby cries. If a mother must work outside of her home, attachment parenting proponents suggest that she simply carry her baby to work in an appropriate sling—a dignified pinstripe sling if she works on Wall Street; a lightweight silk sling if she is a paratrooper; or a bulletproof sling with built-in holster if she is a policewoman.

Attachment parenting frequently involves "baby-led weaning," which means that infants are breast-fed until they naturally lose interest in it, which tends to occur somewhere between two and seven years of age. If children have not developed an interest in solid food by that point, desperate measures are sometimes called for:

Breakfast

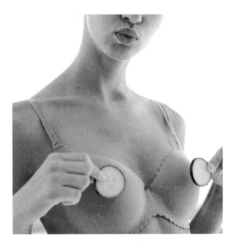

Lunch

Dinner

An added advantage of surgically attaching your infant daughter's skull to your own: You don't need to worry about her abandoning you in your old age.

Some advocates of attachment parenting even forbid the use of teddy bears, security blankets, or other "luvvies," because these "transitional objects" serve as substitutes for parental contact. These parents believe that nothing is more important than establishing a safe and trusting relationship with your child, even if you have to rip the security blanket out of their tiny trembling arms to do it.

As always, our advice when weighing conflicting opinions is to carefully consider the arguments advanced by all sides, and then just take the most extreme position humanly possible. We therefore suggest that, rather than maintaining frequent physical contact with your baby, you *never put him down, ever.*

— — — — — — — —

CHAPTER 8

The Toddler Years: From "No No No" to "NO NO NO NO NO NO!"

Congratulations! You, and possibly your spouse and your child, have survived the first year. Your child is no longer a baby but a toddler—a word derived from the ancient Greek root *todlos,* meaning "No! I won't! You can't make me! NO NO NO NO NO NO NO NO NO NO NO NO NO NO! NO NO! NO!"[1]

Behavior Modifications

There are countless methods of discipline, from positive reinforcement to carefully thought out punishments. Your toddler will use all of these techniques to mold you like warm putty.

---

1   Ancient Greek was a remarkably compact language.

TECHNIQUE	HOW YOUR TODDLER WILL USE IT	HOW YOU CAN RESIST IT
Positive reinforcement	Give you an adorable smile when you do what he wants	Keep your eyes closed at all times.
Reverse psychology	Reject your offer of food or a toy until you offer more food or a better toy	Just offer her the good stuff right away, because you're going to end up doing it anyway.
Time-outs	Completely ignore Mom whenever Dad is around	Divorce husband and marry another woman. How about that, kiddo? Now whichever parent you choose, it's going to be Mommy. I showed you!

"Look into my eyes. You are getting verrrrrry sleepy. Soon, you will believe that broccoli is a sometimes food."

Disciplining Your Child

The toddler years are a time for a child to test limits—in particular, the limits of your patience, the limits of your endurance, and the limits of your pocketbook. Toddlers need rules in much the same way they need expensive heirlooms: as something to shatter into a million pieces.

Here are some techniques for steering your child away from destructive behavior and toward other, equally destructive behavior that you can at least feel you have a say in:

- *Offer your child choices.* If you simply tell your child, "It's time to get dressed," she is likely to just say "No." If, by contrast, you say, "Would you like to wear the red shirt or the blue shirt?" she will have to say "No" twice, providing her lungs with twice as much exercise.

It took eight months of around-the-clock surveillance, but at long last, Jenkins had finally caught his son being good.

- *Catch your child being good.* Experts say that positive reinforcement is much more effective than negative reinforcement. Rather than say "Stop hitting Mommy's vase with that hammer," try saying, "Oooh! Look at all the things you didn't hit with a hammer!" (Note: This only works if there is anything left in your house that has not been hit with a hammer.)

- *Avoid situations that are likely to lead to a tantrum,* such as staying inside, going outside, trying to put your child down to sleep before he is tired, waiting too long to put him down and letting him get overtired, speaking to him, not speaking to him, giving him too many toys, not giving him enough toys, or breathing.

- *Reward charts:* Create a chart with a line for each day of the week. Every day that your child displays the desired behavior, put a sticker on the

appropriate line. Then, when they've accumulated enough stickers, give them a reward, such as more stickers, which they can collect until they have enough to trade in for more stickers, which you can put on the chart to start the process again. Think of stickers as toddler crack, yourself as the pusher, and the reward chart as the pimped-out Mercedes in which you cruise their neighborhood.

Elissa awoke from a twenty-four-hour good-behavior bender with an odd itchy feeling on her cheeks and forehead.

- *Distract your child before trouble starts.* If you see your toddler heading for something breakable, distract him by breaking it yourself first. Nothing you can do can prevent your one-year-old from destroying a four-hundred-year-old porcelain vase, so you might as well have the fun of smashing it yourself.

Bath Time

A nice bath is the perfect way for your toddler to prepare for bedtime. As you watch her relaxing and splashing in warm, soothing water, you will feel yourself relaxing, too, as the stress of your own day fades away. Publishing technology currently prevents us from installing a siren in these pages, so we will simply say: **WAKE UP!** A child in a bath requires your complete attention at all times. Children can drown in as little as 1/10,000,000th of a millimeter of water in half the time it takes a hypercaffeinated hummingbird to flap a pair of spring-loaded wings.

In fact, to be as safe as possible, we recommend you keep your child away from even microscopic moisture. The simplest way to do this is to add an ordinary industrial-strength dehumidifier to the plastic bubble in which you have already placed them. If, for some reason, you have chosen to let your children run free, you will need to hire a corps of highly trained moisture-removal technicians to follow them at all times, swooping in with an organic cotton towel the instant a bead of sweat appears on their brow.

Even better, we recommend moving to Chile's Atacama Desert, the driest region on Earth, where entire millennia pass without a single drop of rain. As an added bonus, the lack of moisture is so extreme there that even the cyanobacteria that thrive in other deserts cannot survive, which means fewer runny noses.

"No, Timmy, don't touch that! Hidden under a cactus's seemingly arid surface is a reservoir of toddler-killing water!"

Toilet Training

Toilet training doesn't have to be stressful. It's simply a battle of wills regarding the control of muscles located inside your child's body, which takes place when he is at the most stubborn stage in human development, and which, if it goes wrong, will result in your kid growing up to be this guy:

Fortunately, the trauma of toilet training can be greatly reduced, as long as you follow our simple tips exactly, and completely disregard any advice from anybody else.

- Buy a high-tech potty that plays soothing classical music as soon as your child tinkles. This creates a positive feedback loop in your child's mind, although it may result in their one day requiring adult diapers to attend a symphony orchestra performance.

- When using words to describe your child's private parts, speak casually, as if you were describing any other part of the body. Children can sense tension in your voice, and it may lead them to think of their genitals as being dirty or shameful. So, for God's sake, whatever you do, don't think about the fact that the slightest hint of tension in your inflection can irreparably damage your child's mental health. In particular, don't think about that photo on the last page of the guy who can't pee unless he's wearing a bull costume, because what probably happened was that his mom one time said "penis" while she was feeling a little stressed, and now the poor guy is so ashamed of his genitalia that he has to cover his entire body before he can urinate. If you're worried you're going to think about it, just repeat "Don't think about bulls when you say 'penis'" over and over and over again.

- Some experts believe that modern diapers make toilet training more difficult, by being so absorbent that children do not experience the sensation of having wet themselves. Instead of diapers, wrap your toddler's bottom in a single square of generic-brand toilet tissue, and then, just to be safe, squirt them repeatedly with a squirt gun.[2]

---

2   You may feel this contradicts our earlier comments regarding the deadly drowning possibilities inherent of even a single molecule of water. You are correct. Nobody ever said parenting was going to be easy.

Or you can just try this.

Pets

A pet is a wonderful addition to your household if you wish to teach your child about compassion and loyalty, or if you feel you simply aren't dealing with enough poop.

Doctors used to warn that early exposure to pets could cause allergies. Newer evidence suggests that early exposure to pets may, in fact, *prevent* allergies. To be safe, we recommend that you own a pet and don't own a pet, simultaneously. This is possible thanks to the new How Not to Kill Your Baby™ Saf-Tee Products Brand© Schrodinger's Pet Cat in a Box, available in pet stores and nuclear physics laboratories near you.

If you have an insurance policy that can be invalidated by the presence of quantum paradoxes inside your home, you will need to consider an alternative. Here are the pros and cons of several common pets.

Pros: *Gentle; easy to care for.*
Cons: *Annual laying of chocolate-filled eggs increases risk of diabetes.*

Pros: *Will remain ever faithful and patient.*

Cons: *Won't teach your child about the cruelty and fickleness of the world.*

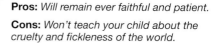

Pros: *Will remain ever faithful and patient, as long as you keep the food coming.*

Cons: *Will eat entire family if you lose the can opener.*

Pros: *Unusual choice may launch child on a lifetime of curiosity and scientific discovery.*

Cons: *Unusual choice may launch child on a lifetime of being the kind of person who keeps a pet snake.*

Pros: *Long-lived. Highly intelligent. Capable of stomping playground bullies into mush.*

Cons: *None.*

Finally given the opportunity to make a friend, the Kutner twins set in motion a plan to trap and keep him for-ever.

CHAPTER 9

Childhood's Halcyon Days, and Other Terrors Beyond Imagining

A s your son or daughter leaves the toddler years behind and begins to enter childhood, a whole new set of challenges begins to present itself. It is an age when your kids worry about their own mortality, get bullied, lie to you, experience peer pressure, and require stitches, frequently all at once. On the other hand, in a few years, they'll be teenagers, at which point they'll be doing all those things *while having sex*. So relax and enjoy your final few years without grandchildren.

Playdates

Since your precious baby was born, you have successfully kept him away from the inferior, disease-filled offspring of other parents. Now, however, your child may begin to display an unfortunate interest in other human beings. You can postpone playdates for some time by convincing your son or daughter that other children are just animated films being projected on tiny fast-moving screens. Ultimately, though, one of them will hit, hug, or blow their nose on your child, and the jig will be up.

Fortunately, playdates can be reasonably safe and only mildly unpleasant, providing you follow these tips:

- To build your own child's sense of self-esteem, slip the other child a fiver and tell him to take a dive at Chinese Checkers.[1]

- Don't just view playdates as a chance for your child's social development. They also build your own character, by forcing you to talk to the other parents about sporting events or celebrities you have no real interest in.

- To make sure that you and the other parents share the same values, have them fill out a playdate application (page 103).

- Before agreeing to a playdate, don't demand to see more than eight years of documented credit history from the other parents. There's no need to be overcautious.

---

1   Then, to turn a profit on the morning, bet the other parent ten dollars that your child will win.

Playdate Application

Parents' names: _____

Mother's maiden name: _____

If mother has kept her maiden name, why?

_____ Has established professional history under maiden name.

_____ Believes women have the right to maintain their own identities.

_____ Plans on divorcing husband soon, leaving their children emotional wrecks who will be terrible influences on their friends.

Do you love your child?

_____ Yes, and like you, I have purchased and committed to memory *How Not to Kill Your Baby*.

_____ No.

How do you intend to prevent your no-good son from becoming an alcoholic and dragging my own precious angel down with him?

_____ By letting him have small amounts of alcohol at home, to de-glamorize alcohol and teach
him how to drink responsibly.

_____ Ha ha! I'm just kidding! No, obviously, I'm going to warn him that alcohol is a gateway drug
to crack cocaine, and then I'm going to tell him I never want to see him drinking, and then
I'm going to hide my own alcohol bottles at the bottom of the trash where he can't possibly
find them unless he knocks over the can or something.

_____ Scientology.

Films

As your child's attention span lengthens and his ability to follow complex stories grows, he will finally reach a milestone you have long dreamed of: You'll be able to plop him in front of a movie and leave him there for two hours.

Be careful, though. Many seemingly harmless films can cause substantial psychological damage.

FILM	LASTING PSYCHOLOGICAL CONSEQUENCES
Bambi	Inability to enjoy great American sport of hunting.
Star Wars	None initially, but you will eventually have to sit down and have "The Talk" about Jar Jar Binks.
The Wizard of Oz	Fortunately, witch-melting scene will inculcate lifelong fear of water, thereby saving child from the deadly risks of bath time. Unfortunately, film will also inculcate lifelong fear of flying monkeys, which could have fatal consequences if child is trapped in burning building with nobody around to rescue him but flying monkeys.
Watership Down	Too many to list.

Reading

Books can activate your child's imagination, touching him on the level of his most primal emotions as well as his most sophisticated thoughts. This makes them even more dangerous than movies.

Decades later, Edna's parents would wish they had never read her Harold and the Purple Crayon.

Fortunately, How Not to Kill Your Baby™ Sayf-Tea Brand© Publishing offers a line of classic children's books, carefully edited to remove anything that could stimulate your child's dangerous sense of wonder.

Sayf-Tea Brand© Peter Pan eliminates all references to flying, which might inspire children to jump out of windows. Instead, Peter Pan and the Darling children jump up and down on a mattress, after having a grown-up remove it from the bed and place it safely on the floor.

Sayf-Tea Brand© *Charlotte's Web* is exactly the same as the original work until the very end, when Charlotte the Spider explains that she was only pretending to be dead, and then she joins Old Yeller, Bambi's mother, and a fully intact Giving Tree in a heart-warming song called "Imagining Things Makes You Sad."

Sayf-Tea Brand© *The Wizard of Oz* consists of twenty-three nonfiction chapters about proper safety precautions during tornado season, followed by the words "And then Dorothy woke up, having learned a valuable lesson about proper safety precautions during tornado season."

Sayf-Tea Brand© *Tom Sawyer* and *Sayf-Tea Brand*© *Huckleberry Finn* don't merely remove all racial epithets, as some of our competitors' editions do. They remove race *entirely*, transferring the story to an all-white suburb of Phoenix, Arizona, in the present day. Don't miss the classic scene where Tom Sawyer tricks his friends into updating his Facebook wall for him!

*Alice receives an important message from
the Mentally Challenged Hatter.*

Nursery School

Having tested the waters of human contact with a playdate, you may eventually need to send your child to school. This means exposing him not merely to germs but to the corrupting influence of other people's opinions. Fortunately, there is one unmistakable bright side: Until your child is being graded on a regular basis, you cannot know for sure whether or not you are winning.

When choosing a nursery school, make sure to visit first, and ask the teachers about their educational philosophies. Then ask about their criminal records. If they insist they have none, you may need to keep asking, perhaps while shining a bright light in their face. Also, take their fingerprints, then follow them home from a discreet distance and go through their trash. Oh, and don't forget to thank them for their dedication to helping the young!

Once you have assured yourself that the teachers aren't terrorists, baby eaters, or, God forbid, union members, it's time to ask about the activities on offer. At the earliest age, "school" activities mostly consist of drawing with crayons and playing in the sandbox. You must therefore assure yourself that the school provides a carefully steam-sanitized sandbox, as well as crayon substitutes made out of corner-free, non-eyebrow-gouging cotton dipped in dyes squeezed from organic fruit. Be sure to do a further criminal background check on any on-site fruit squeezers.

Of course, the attitude of the staff toward children is much more important than the quality of the crafts materials. Are all children praised equally for their efforts and encouraged to express their creativity for its own sake? If so, withdraw your child immediately and find a school where his work will be clearly identified as the best. Even better, try to find a school where other children are publicly ridiculed for not being as good as your son or daughter.

Lastly, and most important, ask about results. Do graduates of this nursery school get into the kindergartens that get kids into the elementary schools that get kids into the middle schools that get kids into the high schools that get kids into the colleges that get kids into good medical schools? Because without a good medical school, recent graduates don't get the kind of residencies that get them the high-paying positions that subsidize the comfortable pension accounts that pay for the luxury assisted living communities that feed into the prestigious nursing homes that have contacts at the top-rated hospices that can get you into the very best cemetery plots. And doesn't your child deserve the best?

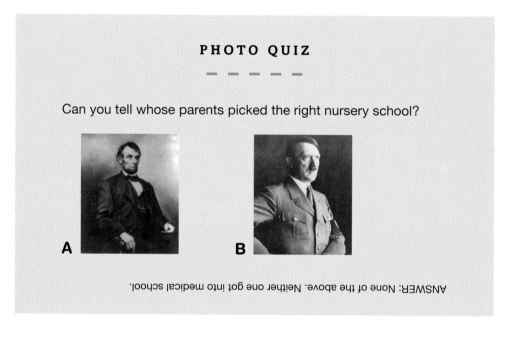

PHOTO QUIZ

- - - - -

Can you tell whose parents picked the right nursery school?

A   B

ANSWER: None of the above. Neither one got into medical school.

Older Children

"Childhood" is a broad term, covering everything from the fresh-out-of-toddlerhood four-year-old to the almost-a-teenager tween. Fortunately, it is easy to adjust your parenting techniques as your children grow: Simply do and say the exact same things, but raise your voice by one decibel for every year of your child's age.

AFTERWORD

If you have made it this far, congratulations! You have successfully maneuvered your children through the open door that is birth and down the winding path of childhood, right into the road where they can be hit by the out-of-control gas truck that is adolescence.

The risks and rewards of the teenage years are far too many and too complex for this book to go into. Instead, we recommend you purchase the companion volume, *How Not to Kill Your Teenager Even If He Deserves It.*

Once your child has made it to adulthood, they will face just as many dangers, but now you will have absolutely no control over them, unless you have taken the sensible precaution of ridiculing them throughout their youth, leaving them without the self-confidence to fend for themselves, and forcing them to move in with you. Otherwise, here is a brief overview of their future. Good luck!

Age/Major Risks

Age 22: *Peak risk of law school.*

Age 21–30: *Unemployability. Marriage to somebody nowhere near good enough.*

Being mugged while on way home to a tiny walk-up in a bad part of a big city far away from you while pursuing dream of a career as a feminist post-grungifunk fire juggler.

Age 37: *Peak risk of really bad comb-over.*

Age 31–39: *Heart attack. Baldness (for men). Marriage to somebody even worse, because you dissuaded them from marrying somebody who wasn't good enough in their twenties, and now after a decade of being picky, all the good ones are taken.*

Age 43: *Peak risk of making comb-over even worse by driving around in a convertible.*

Age 40–49: *Divorce. Gradually dawning realization that he or she will never be elected president.*

Age 54: *Peak risk of gentle, reflective melancholy.*

Age 50–59: *Assassination (if previous realization turned out to be wrong).*

Age 65: *Peak risk of forwarding e-mails because they say "FORWARD TO EVERYONE YOU KNOW!!!" in subject line.*

Age 60–69: *Baldness (for women).*

Age 77: *Peak risk of driving too slowly on highway, causing aneurism in brain of angry 43-year-old in convertible behind you.*

Age 70–120: *Whatever hasn't killed them already.*

Age 100: *Peak risk of appearance on the Today show.*

Age 120+: *Reanimation by evil genius, followed by final destruction when zombie army narrowly fails to conquer Earth.*

Official How Not to Kill Your Baby™ Saqfe-Tqy© Power Decoys

Cut out the following images and glue them on the walls throughout your home.

As an added safety measure, glue the following images over all actual sockets:

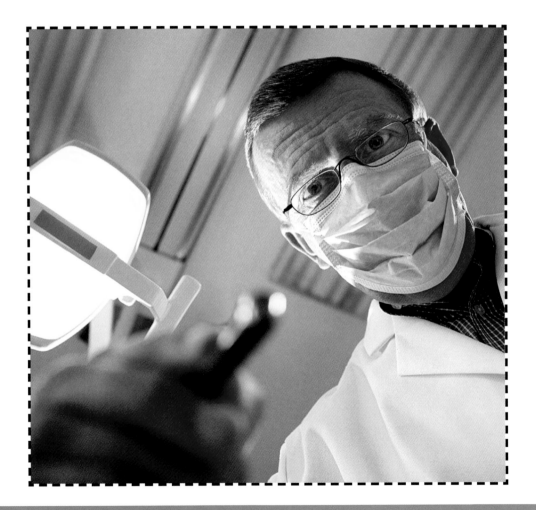

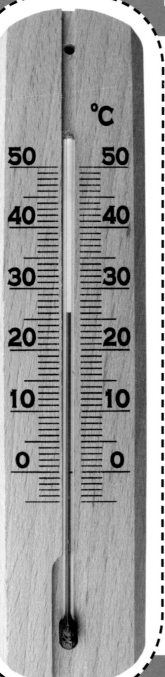

Official How Not to Kill Your Baby™ Saqfe-Tqy© Bath Thermometer

Just clip and remove! Then hold above bathwater. If paper combusts, steam has been superheated to 451° Fahrenheit, and is probably not safe for baby. (*Important note*: Measurement of lower temperatures may require traditional thermometer.)

END USER LICENSE: By purchasing, reading, and/or opening this book, you agree that you have read and will comply with all relevant safety warnings, and you agree to hold the author of this book, as well as his editor, agent, publisher, and dedicatees, entirely harmless in the case of any damage or loss, whether accidental or through negligence, even if they break into your house in the middle of the night and steal all your stuff. Furthermore, you acknowledge the contributions of the following people, and promise that on your next encounter with them, you will buy them a pint of beer or a cup of tea, or maybe some kind of crazy English boilermaker where you fill a cup with tea and then drop it into a beer mug. Most importantly, you recognize that anything that is offensive, inaccurate, or unfunny in this book is entirely the author's fault, and, in fact, the people below probably tried to persuade him to delete it and nearly broke off their friendship when he refused.

WARNING: At this point, the book stops being funny and starts being sincere to a possibly awkward degree.

For reading an earlier draft and offering feedback, suggestions, and some of the funniest jokes in the book: Matthew David Brozik, Steven D'Ambrose, Larry Doyle, Teme Ring, Beth Schacter, and Sheryl Zohn. For Japanese translation services, Mayumi Negishi. For making the book look great, Diane Marsh and Julie Barnes. For their enthusiastic support and sound advice on this and many other projects: my agent, Robert Shepard, and my editor, Lane Butler. For enabling me to focus on my writing because I knew my daughter was in excellent hands, Lore.

For demonstrating that great parents can retain a sense of humor about the whole thing, my mom and dad, to whom this book is dedicated.

For her love and support in absolutely everything, my wife, Lauren. For being awesome, our children, Erin and Joseph.

IMAGE CREDITS

Note: All photos are posed photographs using models. Captions are for strictly humorous purposes and do not reflect any actual activities or characteristics of photo subjects.

Page v, vi:
iStockphoto/Thinkstock

Page 4:
Hemera/Thinkstock

Page 5:
Photos.com/Thinkstock

Page 6:
Polka Dot RF/Thinkstock

Page 8:
iStockPhoto/Thinkstock
Ryan McVay/Photodisc/Thinkstock
Jupiterimages

Page 7:
iStockPhoto/Thinkstock

Page 10 (and all other instances of Dan's Tips for Dads/Dads-to-Be):
iStockphoto

Page 14:
Jeffrey Hamilton

Page 15:
iStockPhoto/Thinkstock

Page 16:
Ken Hammond/ARS
Scott Bauer/ARS
John Foxx

Page 17:
Stockbyte
Jupiterimages

Page 18:
Barbara Penoyar/Thinkstock
Jupiterimages/Thinkstock

Page 20:
NASA

Page 21:
iStockPhoto/Thinkstock

Page 24:
Hemera/Thinkstock

Page 26:
George Doyle and Ciaran Griffin

Page 27:
NASA

Page 29:
iStockPhoto/Thinkstock
iStockPhoto/Thinkstock
Photodisc

Page 30, 31:
Creatas
Hemera/Thinkstock

Page 32:
Water bottle: iStockphoto/Thinkstock
Baby: Jupiterimages

Page 34:
Baby: Jupiterimages
Can: iStockphoto/Thinkstock

Page 35:
Microscopic virus and blue cushion:
iStockphoto/Thinkstock
Green ornament pillow and red striped
pillow: Hemera/Thinkstock

Page 36:
Kids: Stockbyte

Page 37:
iStockphoto/Thinkstock

Page 40:
NASA

Page 42:
NASA

Page 44:
Hemera/Thinkstock

Page 45:
Hemera/Thinkstock

Page 49:

iStockphoto/Thinkstock

Jupiterimages

iStockphoto/Thinkstock

Jupiterimages

iStockphoto/Thinkstock

Page 50:

Jupiterimages

Page 52:

Hemera Technologies

Page 57:

iStockphoto/Thinkstock

Page 59:

iStockphoto/Thinkstock (modified by author)

Page 60:

Medioimages/Photodisc

Page 61:

Hemera/Thinkstock

Page 63:

iStockphoto/Thinkstock

iStockphoto/Thinkstock

Page 64:

Hemera/Thinkstock

Page 65:

Still from *Nosferatu* courtesy of Internet Archive (archive.org).

Page 70:

Marc Debnam

Page 72:

iStockphoto

Page 78:

iStockphoto/Thinkstock

Page 80:

iStockphoto/Thinkstock

Page 83:

Thinkstock Images

Thinkstock

Page 84:

Rayes

Page 87:

iStockphoto

Jupiterimages

Thinkstock Images

Page 88:

iStockphoto/Thinkstock

Page 91:
iStockphoto/Thinkstock

Page 92:
iStockphoto/Thinkstock

Page 93:
iStockphoto/Thinkstock

Page 94:
iStockphoto/Thinkstock

Page 95:
Ryan McVay

Page 97:
Jupiterimages

Page 98:
iStockphoto/Thinkstock
Jupiterimages

Page 99:
iStockphoto/Thinkstock
Hemera Technologies
Erik Snyder

Page 100:
Jupiterimages

Page 105:
iStockphoto/Thinkstock

Page 106:
Original image by Sir John Tenniel; scan by
oldbookart.com; modified by author

Page 108:
Library of Congress
Photos.com

Page 111:
Hemera/Thinkstock

Page 112:
Hemera/Thinkstock

Page 113:
Thinkstock Images

Page 114:
iStockphoto/Thinkstock

Page 115:
iStockphoto/Thinkstock

INDEX

---- ---- ---- ---- ---- ---- ---- ----

G

grapes, pesticide covered, 16

Greenblatt-Gutierrez, Asadkljhrw3rw, 37

Grzbclik, Ernesto, 78

H

hands, freakishly large, 52

Harvard, likelihood that graduate is a
    convicted criminal, 26

hats, 69

Hitler, Adolf, 108

I

immaculate conception, staggering risks
    of, 3

implanting your spawn in chest of innocent
    spaceman, likelihood of leading to
    mortal encounter with Sigourney
    Weaver, 3

IVF, terrifying outcomes of, 3

J

Jones, Don'tBotherMeIJustWantAFrickin
    Shower, 37

K

kidnappers
    apprehended by deaf policemen, 80
    thwarted by cleverly written birth
        announcement, 39

L

labor
    compared to a python devouring a
        Great Dane, 48
    dangerous baby eaters who try to stop
        you from panicking about, 47
    discomfort during, 46
    frantically hailing a cab during, 46
    linked to hair loss, black eyes, and
        broken tailbones, when done right,
        63
    usefulness of a quarter-scale model of
        the U.S. House of Representatives
        in, 48
    when eighty feet tall, 49

letter "e," risks to vision of, 19

Lincoln, Abraham, as disappointment to
    his parents, 108

M

malpractice attorney, present at birth, 44

marriage, probably false and leading to
    eternal damnation, 9

mastadons, ultimately interfering with
    safety-seat installation, 56

medical personnel
    addicted to crack, 26
    addicted to crystal meth, 26
    addicted to heroine, 26
    addicted to porn, 26

ABOUT THE AUTHOR

Credit: Randy Sager

Jacob Sager Weinstein and his wife live in London with their two children, neither of whom has ever been lost at sea or stuck in the middle of a buffalo stampede. Also, that one time he wasn't paying attention and the baby carriage got blown into the Regent's Park Duck Pond, neither of his children was in it.